EARN TRUST

By Changing Selling Into Helping

Practical Tips For Client Development & Networking

James W. Barratt

Book•nol•o•gy

n. delivering useable information and knowledge
that adds value to people's lives

A Business And Educational Imprint From Adducent

EARN TRUST | BY CHANGING SELLING INTO HELPING

Practical Tips For Client Development & Networking

James W. Barratt

ISBN: 9781937592950

Published by BOOKNOLOGY (a business and educational imprint from Adducent).

Jacksonville, Florida

www.AdducentCreative.com

DISCLAIMER: This guidebook is inspired by the author's professional work experience, events, and people relating to those events. And these have been crafted as a business fable intended to discuss and explain relevant expertise and activities, but this construct—the story—is a product of the author's imagination where names, characters, and locations have been used fictitiously. All statements of fact, opinion, or analysis expressed are those of the author. They do not reflect the official positions or views of the publisher. Nothing in the contents should be construed as asserting or implying authentication of information or endorsement of the author's views. This book and subjects discussed herein are designed to provide the author's opinion about the subject covered and is for informational purposes only.

TABLE OF CONTENTS

DEDICATION & ACKNOWLEDGMENTS

To all the people who throughout my life have taught, helped, and believed in me so that I am empowered and encouraged to strive to help others.

Many of us have said to ourselves someday, I will write a book. Well, for me, that day has arrived.

This journey began long before I even thought about sharing my observations with others. I am fortunate to have had such a great career so far, and there were many fits and starts as well as painful and rewarding lessons. I am grateful to so many people in my personal and professional life who have taught, influenced, supported, and helped me along the way. I give thanks for:

My loving and supporting parents, George A. Barratt, Jr. and Norma Jean Barratt, who instilled in me a moral compass, a drive to achieve, and the importance of kindness.

My sister, Susan Sullivan, and my brothers George, Michael, and Thomas Barratt, who taught me growing up that you need to work hard to get what you want, and the importance of staying connected and sharing unconditional love and support.

My children, Grace, Emma, and Jackson, you generate in me the most profound feelings of pride, joy, and love that sustain and motivate me every day to always do my best. You each possess unique gifts and talents the world will no doubt benefit from in your promising futures. Your mother, Venus Bazan Barratt, is an amazing role model for you, and I am so grateful for her support over the years.

My extended family of in-laws, nieces and nephews and grandnieces and grandnephews who are bringing along a new generation of children who inspire and entertain.

My colleagues. My professional career has been an interesting series of passages from one experience to the next, which has allowed me to grow personally and professionally and create a fantastic network of friends, colleagues, and clients.

My fellow non-profit board members and staff.

My writing collaborator, Dennis Lowery.

Some of my friends, colleagues, and clients who have encouraged me along the way (listed alphabetically):

Ama Adams
Tamela Aldridge
Steve Bachman
Tom Bechtel
Brad Bennett
Alex Bourelly
Steven I. Butler
Bruce Carton
Jeff Clark

Jane Cobb
Tamara Copeland
Stephen Crimmins
Patrick Dennis
Jim Doty
Palmina Fava
Jason Flemmons
Joe Gardemal
Dan Goelzer
Ilsy Hoo
Yousr Khalil
Joe Lombard
Brian McDowell
Mark McGrath
Frances McLeod
Susan Markel
Daniel Nathan
Charlotte Y. Reid
Steve Richards
Carla Rosati
SEC Historical Society
Only Make Believe
Operation Understanding DC
Leadership Greater Washington
Liz Wainger
Joe Walker
F. Joseph Warin
Martin Weinstein
David Whitmore
Marty Wilczynski

And I give thanks to God.

Foreword

I have been in the business world for 50 years now, starting my career as a banker and then moving into professional services. For the last fifteen years, I've owned my own consulting practice. I met Jim Barratt in 1997, over twenty years ago, when I hired him to work with me to start and manage a forensic consulting practice at the office of a national accounting firm. We also worked together at one of the "Big Four" accounting firms.

In *Earn Trust*, Jim shares some of the lessons he has learned over the years from his work in professional services. This book will help others who may face some of the same issues and challenges both Jim and I encountered throughout our careers.

Jim's insights are not based on theories learned in business school. They come from his experience as an accountant and consultant to many clients over many years. The reader would do well to trust and consider the advice Jim offers. This book is written in a style that makes it more of a conversation than a textbook; as you read this book, you will be mentored, not lectured.

Many of the points that Jim addresses are critical to success in the business world, where everyone is selling something. And that success comes more often when we help our clients. For example, we need to listen to our clients and prospective clients to realize the opportunities being offered. We need to determine and manage expectations, develop relationships, make connections, commit to ongoing communication, and gather and act on feedback. But most of all, we need to help our clients. That's how we earn trust, and that's what builds our foundation for success.

Read the book, as I did, and you'll have a better understanding of how to help your clients... and to create and maintain a productive and rewarding professional career.

Steven I. Butler, CFE, Owner,

Brittany Consulting, LLC

"Stories are remembered up to 22 times more than facts alone." When people think of advocating for their ideas, they think of convincing arguments based on data, facts, and figures. However, studies show that if you share a story, people are often more likely to be persuaded. And when data and story are used together, audiences are moved both intellectually and emotionally. When telling a story, you take the listener on a journey, moving them from one perspective to another. In this way, story is a powerful tool for engendering confidence in you and your vision.

—Stanford Graduate School of Business

INTRODUCTION

In my career, I've learned the importance of earning trust and how one way to attain it is by helping others. HELP: the origin of the word has such meanings as to support, to benefit, to do good, to cure. I like to think of HELP as standing for How to Eliminate Life's Problems. That philosophy has worked for me, and I think it is good advice for others, no matter your profession or career. Some problems and situations covered in this book are ones most professionals contend with, including:

- Just not enough time to do what needs to be done.

- Being uncomfortable/unsure about how to interact with clients in a business development setting.

- Client discussions about your competition and how you are different.

- Overcoming complacency or just plain laziness.

- Handling the confusion resulting from a crisis or confrontation.

- Uncertainty about a direction or action to take.

This is a business book about furthering your career, which presumably, and naturally, also means making more money and becoming more secure professionally. Within this book, I use HELP as a means by which you discover how it—helping—is an excellent path to earning trust. And that is a cornerstone to better 'selling.' It is a guidebook for mid-career and experienced professionals to create a valuable network and develop new business opportunities for themselves and the companies that employ them.

If you work to view client development activities to help people and not something to fear or dislike, you can earn trust and grow into a successful client developer. So, turn from a focus on selling—pitching clients—to helping them, and that will lead to new and, often, repeat clients.

While I hope the ideas in this book will help advance your career, it must be said that if a client does not trust or have respect for you or does not think you do an excellent job on their projects, then whatever networking and client development steps you take will not matter. It is too late if you have lost the confidence of your client. Ensuring that you are meeting and exceeding the client's expectations is the primary factor in maintaining your status as a trusted advisor.

To be a successful consultant requires a myriad of skills and abilities. Which include but are not limited to technical expertise, strong communication skills, responsiveness, reliability, analytical and creative thinking, ability to manage processes and people, likeability, commitment to the work, efficiency, and the list goes on. Successful professionals typically have a mix of most of the required traits. A skilled professional develops self-awareness of their strengths and weaknesses and works to improve themselves and their colleagues.

To illustrate how this plays out in the real world, parts of this book are presented in the form of a story—a series of vignettes—about a successful seasoned executive, John, and the successful protégé he sold his company to, Sophia, and two younger executives, Mark and Stephanie. I hope presenting my decades of experience as scenes with dialog or within correspondence between the four characters delivers the tips and guidance in a better—more relatable—way.

What you're about to read was written mainly pre-COVID-19 and the 2020 pandemic. Still, the core of the advice is valid and valuable despite the changes our world has experienced. COVID-19 has changed how we work. Events have required many to adapt to different and new ways of performing their work. We have replaced much of our routine business travel and physical interaction with virtual meetings. And activity has increased on a range of digital platforms to facilitate—remote, but still personal—connectivity so crucial in business.

During these extraordinary times, millions have had to shift to work remotely, and that could become the future for jobs that need not be performed at a specific business location. The COVID-19 pandemic has made many people question long-established beliefs about the 'way things are done.' Though the discussion about the implications of technology's impact on the workplace has long been underway. Business and professional performance needs, and practical—actual—requirements, are now under scrutiny as they have never been before. The pandemic has made one thing markedly clear: the future of work and the workplace for many professionals is no longer pre-determined. Flexibility and adaptability will determine where and how we work in six months, a year, or a decade from now. The tools we're using because of COVID-19 and the pandemic can be adopted and adapted to follow the advice in this book regarding client and business development engagement.

OPENING

JOHN'S HOME

His cell phone rang loudly in the quiet house. Too quiet, John thought, and it made almost every moment exponentially add to how much he missed Sarah. The house was too big and his life too empty without her. He glanced at the caller ID and was surprised. Not as much at the late hour of the call, but who it was. "Sophia! An unexpected but pleasant caller. How are you?" He walked back into his study, put her on speaker, and set the phone on his desk as he pulled his chair up to sit.

"I'm fine, John... and sorry for the lateness of the call," her voice, a lilting British accent, always conveyed the same dignity she had in person.

"It's good to hear from you. You're welcome to call any time," John heard her take a deep breath and pause before replying. The Sophia Omondi he knew was never hesitant. She had that confident presence others sensed when they met and spoke with her that she understood in advance what she wanted to say and did not dawdle trying to find the words.

"I know we are years past the period of transition, the hand-off and consultancy that was part of the deal when I bought the company from you. But something has come up, and I need your help."

John knew Sophia had aggressively taken his former company into new markets, especially globally. Something he had hesitated to do because he was comfortable with the company size and market he had developed. But then Sophia had more international experience and contacts worldwide than he, and she was younger and more driven. Under her ownership, it had made sense and was a natural progression for the growth of the company. And the last he had heard from her; all was going well. Had there been a stumble, was she or the company in trouble?

"Trouble or a problem with the business?" he asked. Complete retirement to spend time with Sarah was why he had sold the company, and his consulting agreement as part of the purchase had long expired, but he could not help but still care.

"No trouble, but it is a situation that affects the business. One of my professors from University College London and three classmates have asked me to help stand up a new Non-Governmental Organization. The NGO is in Kenya, and they want me to serve as the inaugural Managing Director until it is on its feet operationally. Post-funding that will take eight months, full-time on-site in Nairobi. I have a new vice president, but Susan is about to go on maternity leave. Besides that, she's a little 'green' and needs more experience before I'd feel comfortable with her as acting CEO. So, my problem is I don't have anyone seasoned enough to step in and run the company if I commit to this new NGO."

John heard her take another deep breath, then continue.

"I'm in a bind. Kenya is my birthplace…, and the NGO's focus is on Child Education. The educational initiatives it can support and its funding of them is one of the few ways to reduce child labor abuse and the prostitution endemic to the country. And the exploitation of girls is especially rife; their fate could have been mine. If my parents had not had help, we would never have made it to England. I would not have the education and opportunities that led me to the U.S and getting to work for you, which was the cornerstone of my success. What I have built is upon the foundation you laid. But I need help, so I can help others and do what I can for children in my birth country." She hesitated; it had always been hard for her to ask for help and to trust people, something John had overcome by proving he cared and wanted her to succeed.

"You know the company has grown, and we are doing well," Sophia continued. "But one area I've not done well in is to build a stronger layer of management, other than Susan, under me. I don't have anyone ready, and you are the only one I can think of that's capable of stepping in so I can take on the work for this new NGO."

When Sophia stopped talking, the silence around John grew, and it felt like an air pressure imbalance. He hated the emptiness of things in his life now and knew he had to have something to help him get through Sarah's loss. And what Sophia wanted to do was important. She and his former company needed him. "I'll do it, Sophia. If there's any way I can help you, I will."

This time it was a sigh of relief over the speaker, "Thank you, John. Can you come to meet with me tomorrow?"

"Of course. Email me the new address. With Sarah's illness and then hospice... I never got down there when you invited me to see your new office."

"John, Sarah was a wonderful woman, and again I am so sorry for your loss. Thank you for helping me. Watch for the email shortly, and I'll see you tomorrow."

THE NEW OFFICE

"It's not like the old office, back when you hired me... is it?" Sophia asked, looking at the man beside her on the sidewalk from the parking lot.

John shook his head as his eyes traveled from the ground to the sky. "It's all windows... glass." The eyes lowered, and glasses slipped down his nose. He pushed them back up to study his younger prodigy. "But nice, very modern."

AN HOUR LATER

"Thanks for the tour and the conversation, which was a nice walk down memory lane... but let's talk about the situation, timing, and what you want me to accomplish while you're gone." John stopped beside Sophia, who stood before a door. Unlike the others that were frosted glass, this one was wooden.

Sophia rapped it with the knuckles of her right hand, "For old time's sake when we moved in, I had one office done a bit differently to honor the company's founder." She turned the knob and entered, flicking a light switch on the wall by the door. "I come in here to sit and sometimes think, especially when I have hard decisions to make."

The walls differed from the other offices and areas they had just viewed: Textured and an off-white, an almost pale cream tint. The furniture—each piece—wood, no metal panels or surfaces, the chairs were leather. Behind the desk, on the wall, was a photograph blown up to a large-scale rectangle that spanned the width of the desk. If it had been frameless, it would have blended into the wall. The photo was of a set of carved wooden letters: CSIH positioned on a wall that looked the same as what the framed picture was mounted on.

John scanned the room, "This looks almost exactly…"

"Like your old office… the one you interviewed me in and then—the second time I was in it—you hired me. Your office is where you taught me about that…" Sophia pointed at the large photo, then walked around the desk to it and tapped each letter on the photograph. "That—earn trust by changing selling into helping—is what you used to build, not just a successful career, but this business."

John smiled and nodded. "True, and I'm proud you learned it so well," he turned around to gesture outside the door. "Look what you've accomplished."

"Thanks, but I'm not as good as you at teaching it," Sophia touched each letter again. "Do you remember your onboarding talk? I do."

THE OLD OFFICE: 20 YEARS AGO
Onboarding Sophia

"Sophia, in some ways, we're all salespeople every day and just don't realize it. From an early age, we learn to use our unique skills, talent, and experiences to get what we want and need. At some point, we develop the ability to persuade another person to share with us and give to us. It is a matter of survival. As babies, we cry, loudly and frequently, if we're hungry or need a clean diaper. At other times, we may smile and giggle and find that elicits a favorable response from those in charge of our universe. As children and teenagers, we're likely to be more self-centered and typically put our efforts toward getting what we want and doing what we want. Usually, without too much thought about what the other person(s) may receive or feel in return. Hopefully, somewhere along the way, we develop a sense of compassion for others and the desire to perform selfless tasks whose sole purpose is to benefit others getting nothing in return, other than a good feeling inside. While not all of us can be a Mother Teresa, who dedicates all of our time and energy to helping others, and hopefully, most of us are not so selfish that everything we do is calculated to benefit ourselves regardless of the consequences. But finding a balance between doing what we need to live and succeed while also helping other people get what they want and need can sometimes be an elusive goal that requires challenging skills to develop.

"So, in some shape or form, we all are 'selling' something to other people. We may not call it that, though. It may be delivering babies or UPS packages. It may be painting a house or an artistic masterpiece. It may be serving food at a restaurant or providing life insurance to a family. It may be inviting people to drive the latest automobile or utilize innovative technologies. So regardless of what type of service or product that may be associated with our livelihood, there will always exist a provider and a client or customer who wants or needs it. And ultimately, trusts and financially commits to the provider of their choice. That's the 'sale,' the transaction we all are part of every day of our lives. From a career standpoint, to succeed and flourish in whatever you are selling, it will require some interaction with potential clients.

"Sometimes, the product may sell itself, and there is little interaction required. In other situations, you will be selling yourself and your individual expertise, which will necessitate the development of a level of trust and respect that may require significantly more time and effort. Depending on the services you provide, there may be a vast population of potential customers or clients, or it may be a very specialized skill that is only sought by a smaller niche of society.

"Regardless of the service provided, the successful interaction between the provider and the recipient involves the execution of a variety of tasks. There are many approaches and methods that successful providers of services use to develop client relationships and grow their networks. There is no one set of principles or commandments that a provider can follow every time to engage with clients, and what works for one person will not always work for another. However, by sharing our experiences with client development approaches, we can hopefully work to help each other become more aware and successful in developing clients and getting new work. As we work together, I'll describe and share with you various tips and lessons learned throughout my career to improving client development. While that will help you grow your network of potential clients, it is not a scholarly treatise or a cookbook recipe. I've been blessed to work with many smart and experienced colleagues who have shown me the way and inspired me to grow in my ability to engage clients and ultimately help them." John stood and stepped to one side to point at the sign behind his desk. "Changing selling into the act of helping people early in my career allowed me to overcome my reluctance and discomfort in reaching out to clients to sell them. To earn their trust, I learned how not to be the pitchman or pitchperson that's seen as an intrusion. And that perspective continues to inspire me to focus on helping provide the highest quality and relevant services to those who need and want them."

* * *

John smiled, "Well, I remember the eager young face of the junior executive I had just hired. The focus in your steady eye contact and the body language said it all. I hired you because you wanted to learn how to succeed and knew I could teach you."

Sophia touched each letter in the photo again. "I believe that things happen for a reason. This NGO opportunity revealed the bind I've put myself in by making the company's business development depend on me and my daily involvement in it. In the back of my mind, that's nagged at me. But when you're busy and have so many demands on your time... you never get around to it," she smiled, "you know what that's like, John. But when you hired and taught me what you had learned in the business and all your years of experience, and I applied it... that eased your burden."

"You learned pretty well from me; well enough to grow the business into this..." John gestured again beyond just the office they were in to include the suite of rooms in the new shining building.

"Yes, but I need you to help me develop another... me. I think your willingness to help so I can focus on the NGO for the next eight months, does more than just 'mind the store' for me, as welcome as that is. What you're so good at that you instilled in me, can help develop a couple of young executives we have that can be stars for the company."

"When do you want me to start?"

"Is tomorrow too soon for you? If you can, then I'd plan to leave for Nairobi early next week after introducing and transitioning to you."

CHAPTER 1 –
KNOW YOUR STUFF

If you don't know, ask. You will be a fool for the moment, but a wise man for the rest of your life.
                                    –Seneca the Younger

THE NEW OFFICE
ONBOARDING STEPHANIE AND MARK

"Come in," John motioned at the two chairs in front of his desk. "So, Sophia has briefed you, I'm here to sit in for her over the next several months and manage daily business operations and to help also with your training. I'll be a mentor to guide you."

John studied the two junior executives as they settled in their chairs before his desk. "What I'm going to talk about might be unexpected or seem unusual. But bear with me for a few minutes; I think it's important that I lay out the path ahead for your work here and how you'll learn to perform your duties." He leaned back in his chair. "I remember growing up as a relatively shy young boy who would typically listen more than talk. As I became older and increasingly comfortable expressing myself, I found it easier to engage with people when I felt I was helping them. I found that it made me feel good and provided an inner energy. The first job I had that included a sales component was working in a sporting goods store. It was a small, family-owned store in a small community, so it was a friendly neighborhood environment. While my tasks included stocking inventory, stringing tennis rackets, and ringing up sales, I was also required to sell products to customers. As I became knowledgeable about the sporting goods products we carried and could help people find what they needed, I could overcome my shyness and could better view selling as a way I could help people get what they needed."

"Selling products and selling professional services are different activities, but they are similar. They both require listening to what a customer or client needs, being knowledgeable about the relevant product or service, and engaging in a dialog with the customer about the benefits and use of the product or service."

"There's something I read this morning from Seth Godin; have you heard of him?" John leaned forward and clicked his laptop mouse to 'wake' the screen on his laptop. "I get his updates on email." He slipped his glasses on to read it. "I'll paraphrase this because it's relevant. He talks about how, if you want to make a long-term impact, build a road. How cities that have been around for a long time, many of the buildings at the city's core—from back at its start, its early growth—most, if not all, are no longer there. They've been replaced by new ones. But the roads—the original paths built around communication, transportation, and connecting parts of the city... are largely still there. If you have traveled to European cities, you've probably seen—maybe even walked or driven on—

ancient Roman roads. So, cities—their buildings—evolve and change, but roads... those paths laid down so long ago, are still there... and still serve your purpose. And that is what I want to teach you how to do. Lay a good foundation for your path to success that works for you now and for years to come."

MENTORING SESSION – EARNING TRUST BY HELPING
AFTER A NEW CLIENT PROSPECT MEETING

As they left the conference room, Mark followed John to his office and stopped in the doorway.

"What is it, Mark?" John asked as he sat down, took his glasses off, and set them on the desk by his phone.

"I listened to you at the meeting, but how do you sell someone if you don't start with telling them what we do?"

John peered over his glasses and studied the young man. "How do you know that what we do is what they'll buy?"

"What do you mean? If they're in our target market. Or asked for a meeting or sent a Request For Proposal (RFP)... then they must be interested." Mark seemed annoyed.

John nodded, "That's true, but just telling them what we can do for them is only part of actually making—hopefully making—the sale."

"What else is there?" Mark looked puzzled.

"If we listen to their needs, we can better explain how what we can provide, can help them. When we listen, we learn what questions to ask to get us to that point. If you indulge me for a moment, I will share with you some of my experiences and how I learned the importance of listening. As I began my professional career as an auditor in one of the largest global accounting firms, I learned quite a bit about how to audit, how to work with and manage people, and how to manage engagements. While I had day-to-day contact with various levels of client employees, I wasn't at a senior enough level to be included in client development. Most of those tasks: reaching out to potential clients, developing relationships and presenting proposals, were conducted by the most senior practitioners, primarily partners. So, along with watching them to learn more... one skill I developed in that auditing experience was listening to people. It was vital to listen carefully to the direction provided by my firm's managers and to the answers provided by the client personnel related to accounting matters." John paused, then continued:

ABOUT NETWORKING

"While I met and worked with a variety of colleagues and clients, I did not appreciate the importance of maintaining and growing a network of professional contacts. But I had learned something about myself; a career as an auditor was not a good fit for me. Though I had done well and risen to become an Audit Manager, I accepted a job with the SEC (US Securities and Exchange Commission) as an Enforcement Accountant.

"At the SEC, the matters I worked on were typically handed to me, and there was plenty of work to keep me busy, so there was not a need to exercise any client development muscles. But I was learning—intuitively—the skills I would need for that when it became part of my role with companies I worked with. I had the great fortune to work with a variety of lawyers. I gained exposure to defense attorneys who were representing witnesses in the cases. While I did not really focus on including these contacts into my professional network, I made lasting contacts and friendships, many of whom became the foundation of much of my success when I became a consultant, and they became my potential clients. In my position at the SEC, I could use my accounting and auditing knowledge while learning how to conduct investigations of potential financial fraud and auditor malpractice. An essential aspect of this position was preparing for and taking the testimony of witnesses related to an investigation. That required some specific skills like researching and becoming knowledgeable about all the facts and evidence and preparing an organized outline in anticipation of interviewing the witnesses. Also—and this is an important skill I still apply today—I learned how to best phrase a question for the witness to understand what I was asking. And then, importantly, listening carefully to what the witness said. This listening required me to understand quickly their response and then develop a relevant follow-up question when needed. I recall testimony sessions where a colleague would elicit an answer from the witness and, without listening to the response, would move on to another line of questioning when contained in the witness response was an important, new fact that cried out for a follow-up. That taught me a lesson too. Watch and learn, but also think for yourself about what's right, or that should become a best practice for yourself. So again, listening to customers and potential clients is a critical component of understanding what they are expressing. When you listen—as I've learned through the experience I just mentioned—and ask the right questions, the client or prospect feels your focus is on helping them, not selling them, and they remember it."

MENTORING CAN HAPPEN AT ANY TIME (BE ATTUNED TO IT)

"It's past 5:00 PM on a Friday... what are you doing still here, Stephanie?" John noticed her as he headed to the lobby.

"Thinking... better to do it here than in traffic."

John draped his jacket over the cubicle wall. "What's on your mind?"

Stephanie scratched her chin and looked up. "One thing they tell you... teach you... in school and in articles, is that it's important to network."

"And that sounds like it tastes bad when you say that."

"No, John... I mean, not really, but I don't think I'm any good at it."

"Why do you think that?"

"Because I'd rather be working... delivering... not chatting up people about hiring me... hiring us."

"So, you think networking is really just selling?" John entered the cubicle and set his briefcase on the chair next to Stephanie's desk.

"Isn't it?"

"Not if you do it right, Stephanie."

"What do you mean?"

"Networking is that part of work that leads to bringing in business so you can help get things done for a client. When I began my consulting career as a forensic accountant in the litigation consulting field, I was limited in my client development and network building experience. Up to that point, I had been an auditor, a government investigator, and a manager of projects. I quickly realized that to advance in the consulting field, it was important that besides managing projects, I needed to identify potential clients, engage with them, and try to develop new business opportunities. At the first consulting firm I worked for, I was very fortunate to work with a seasoned practitioner who had been consulting for decades. He showed and taught me so many essential skills and practices required to develop a professional network and identify and be retained on new consulting engagements. I was grateful that he included me in lunch meetings with potential clients and presentations of proposals. As I was learning these valuable insights, I realized that while I was working to build my network and presenting our services to potential clients, at the end of it all, I was trying to help the client. In viewing my work this way, my focus shifted from talking about me and my skills and my firm's experience... listening to the client and what they believed they needed or wanted. Once I had this realization, 'selling' was replaced with the philosophy—and operating principle—of 'helping.' I've found that most people are more comfortable helping others than trying to sell them something. I know I am." John lifted his jacket, "Think about what I said over the weekend, and we can talk more about it."

New Client Prospect Meeting
Managing Expectations By Not Overpromising Or Misrepresenting

"Thanks for your time; this was a good meeting that gives us some insight into how we might help you. And if not, we can give you some ideas or direction." John shook the CEO's hand.

Minutes later in the car, Mark turned to him. "They want to hire us now, he even mentioned how he heard about us from other clients. Why did you tell them we'd need to see how we 'might' be able to help them? Why not tell them we can do it and then figure it out later?"

"You mean fake it till you make it?" John shook his head.

"Well, yeah... something like that."

"You could do that... wing it and maybe even pull it off. But in my experience, it's better to be straight with the client. I remember once the firm I was with had an opportunity to provide services related to an investigation in Latin America, which would require Spanish language reading and speaking skills. While we had the general investigative experience, we did not have a Latin America presence and had minimal Spanish language skills within the firm. So, we reached out to a native Spanish speaking accountant who was doing temporary project work to supplement our team proposal. The law firm representing the client was a well-regarded firm, and the lead partner was a rainmaker there. I was keen on helping them but had some misgivings about presenting a proposal as we were limited in specific areas: the depth of our language skills and geographic presence. I wanted to win the work, but I also wanted to preserve the respect of the law firm partner for future referrals. After some discussion with my partners, we agreed to meet with the law firm to present our qualifications. We had submitted a written qualifications piece before the in-person meeting. The meeting was at the law firm, and there was the rainmaker partner with several of his associates, along with myself and three colleagues. We introduced ourselves and gave a brief statement on our background and relevant experiences.

"The lead partner instantly focused on what our presence was in Latin America. We said that while we did not have offices there, we have conducted investigations in various countries there in the past. They would have wanted a firm that had local people so the costs would be cheaper and where there would be offices, they could stage interviews, etc. The questions we received were direct and straightforward, and I made sure we answered them honestly. When it came to our native language skills, we referenced the sub-contracted native Spanish speaker, and they asked if there was anyone else. We indicated we could add people as needed. However, they likely thought that if we would add people who were not part of our firm, they might be of questionable quality and experience. We highlighted our investigation experience, but it seemed apparent that we were really coming up short of what they were looking for to conduct an extensive investigation in the country. The law firm partner was professional about it, but he mostly thanked us for our time, and we left. I left feeling we had been straight with them as to our capabilities and had not lost our integrity. We soon heard from them they went with someone else, and I thanked them for the opportunity. Because we were honest and transparent with the attorney about our specific capabilities, he has reached out and hired me for other work. That was a real-world experience that taught me, in the long run, it's much better to be straightforward."

They pulled into their parking lot, "Come with me," John waved at Mark to follow to his office. Inside he spotted Stephanie, "Do you have a few minutes?" She nodded, and he continued, "join us then... in my office." They entered, and he sat behind his desk. "I'm going to read my latest email from Sophia to you. It's on an important topic." John picked up the sheet of paper and settled his bifocals:

```
-------- Original Message --------

Subject: the importance of research - from my
journal notes of what you taught me
From: "Sophia Omondi" <sophia.omondi@ePost.net>
Date: April 4
To: "John" <JohnW1949@ePost.net>

John,

I brought my journals with me that contain
the notes I kept from the day you hired
me, and over time have added more of what
I learned from you. This is something you
emphasized, and I took to heart, I'd like you
to discuss with Mark and Stephanie:
```

RESEARCH YOUR FIRM'S CAPABILITIES IF YOU DON'T KNOW THEM

```
Professional services firms vary in size and
```

may employ 20 or 20,000 professionals. You may not always encounter professionals in your firm who practice in different service lines, so you must reach out to others to learn more about what they do. Most colleagues are happy to talk about their practice lines and how they can help clients. By requesting to learn more, you will not only become more knowledgeable about other service lines, but you will now have another internal connection who presumably you will inform about your service offerings, so you have spread your internal network even broader and potentially have additional colleagues who may refer work to you.

Along these lines, you will also want to understand what services your competitors offer. If they compete with your service lines, then you will want to understand how well-positioned they are. It is important to understand your firm's service line strengths and limitations, and those of your competition so you can answer the client's question: "What makes you guys different?" By being familiar with the marketplace, you will be perceived to be an informed professional by your client, and they may regard you as a player in the space who should be listened to. You may also earn points as being an honest broker if you indicate to your client you do not compete in certain services or geographic locations. While you do not want to talk your client out of hiring you, they will respect you more if you assess the expertise you offer and possibly where you can refer them.

John flipped to the next page, "Now, here's my reply, which includes what I want to share with you."

-------- Original Message --------
Subject: a couple of the things I met with
Stephanie and Mark today
From: "John"
Date: April 5
To: "Sophia Omondi"

Sophia,

You kept some great notes. Knowing your own capabilities and those of others that can become an asset to you or your company is critical. Part of understanding capabilities comes out when you get questions asked of you, and you have to be prepared with answers. Here are the questions—you know these already—but I'll go over with Stephanie and Mark in our next meeting:

QUESTIONS FROM CLIENTS

- What type of services do you offer?
- Do you have anyone who is an expert in this kind of matter?
- How many people do you have in your firm? In your practice area?
- Do you have locations in other countries? Which ones?
- We need an estimated budget for this project. What are your hourly billing rates?
- How would you propose we accomplish this task? What is your approach?
- What relevant experience do you have regarding this specific engagement?
- Why should we hire you?
- What makes you different?

Some practitioners will respond to a client's inquiry with: "Of course, we can do that" even when they are pretty sure they can't, but they will then try to cobble together a proposal or presentation that may not pass the 'straight face' test. One way to lose the trust of a client is to present a proposal that does not accurately portray the qualifications and resources that you can bring to a project. You can imagine how upset a client would be if you are retained and cannot execute the task as you presented. You never want to be in that position.

And the above leads to the following that I'll also discuss with Stephanie and Mark:

TUNE IN TO WHAT OTHERS ARE WORKING ON

While you may be very busy with engagements and are deep into your practice expertise, it is helpful to talk with your colleagues to understand what type of work they are doing and for whom. As professionals working in a variety of areas and traveling out of the office frequently, it is sometimes challenging to stay up to speed on other's activities. Depending on your firm's practices, you may be included in distributions of detailed information that indicate potential engagements for which conflict checks are being conducted and actual engagements where your firm was retained. Much of this work may be confidential. Still, you should be able to talk with your colleague about the nature of the work being performed and who the client is. You may find that on potential clients that you have a contact at the client and your participation on the project team or at least having the contact aware that your firm is pitching this work can sometimes be

a valuable addition to a proposal for work.
Again, developing your internal network of
contacts and knowing what your firm offers
and what your colleagues are working on will
help you in becoming a valued resource to
your clients.

Another way to learn what other colleagues
are working on or matters that people in the
firm have worked on in the past is to research
a client relationship management system to
the extent one is available in your firm.
These systems can vary in sophistication, but
what you really need is to know who in the
firm is already a contact of your potential
client and how well do they know them. It is
helpful to know as well if the firm is working
with the client's company or has done work
in the past.

It's helpful to let the potential client know
that you and your firm have worked or currently
are working with their firm. You can reference
colleagues you have worked with, and this can
serve many times as a potential endorsement
of the quality of the work you and your firm
have provided.

John put down the stapled emails and pushed his
glasses higher on his nose. "You might not keep a journal
like Sophia did when she worked for me, but keep notes,"
he nodded at Stephanie's legal pad and noted the flash of
chagrin on Mark's face. "To help, I'll ask Sophia if she's
okay with me giving you copies of emails between her and
me on relevant topics."

POINTS TO THINK ABOUT

Take a moment and reflect on what you've read and consider:

1. How well do you know the services your firm provides?

2. When was your most recent conversation with a colleague regarding their expertise and recent engagements?

3. When was the last time you perused your company website to learn new information?

4. Do you regularly reach out to colleagues to get an understanding of what they are working on?

CHAPTER 2 –
IN YOUR CLIENT'S
SHOES

Most people do not listen with the intent to understand; they listen with the intent to reply.
                                          –Stephen Covey

THE NEW OFFICE
THE NEGATIVE IMPACT OF 'OVER-PITCHING'

"Sometimes, you can talk your way out of a sale, Mark."

"But I wasn't sales pitching them... I was listening like you told us!" Mark looked at Stephanie then back to John. "And then all I did was comment on something they said."

"If a client mentions something bad about anyone... a competitor... a vendor... anyone... let it pass without comment. Don't use that as the opportunity to point out how we're different or better. Never talk so much that you focus more on what you are saying or want to say... and forget to pay attention to who you're meeting with. Watching someone losing that focus cost me a new client once. At a firm I was with, I presented our qualifications in a specific area to several law firm partners who had invited me to their offices. I brought several colleagues with relevant experience. And as I did most of the time when there is a group presentation, I had coordinated with all of my colleagues to plan what we'd highlight and any other considerations to help them. When we met with the attorneys, we went around the room and introduced ourselves and our backgrounds. They did the same and briefed us on their core focus, which was that they represented defendants in this matter and were adverse to the plaintiffs. One of my colleagues latched on to the subject area and had done some work for the plaintiff side. He went off script and was going on at length about the shortcomings of the defenses he had seen. I could see that the attorneys were shifting in their seats, blank expressions turning to frowns... so I tried my best to cut off the colleague and redirect the discussion to give a more balanced view of our collective experience. But the damage was done. Learn from my mistakes and what I share with you from my experience, Mark."

SOMETIMES THE RIGHT PERSON IS NOT THE MOST SENIOR

"Both of you did good work on this proposal," John told Stephanie and Mark. "And Sophia is really pleased." Stephanie smiled, and Mark looked smug. "She asked who I thought should be the lead on the project, and it's clear." Mark straightened and leaned forward. "From what I saw in the planning sessions, Stephanie has the best rapport. She'll take the lead with this client."

Mark slumped; the smug expression replaced by a frown. "What? Why is that? I'm senior to her by months." He glanced at Stephanie, "nothing against you... but I am.

I should—"

"Mark," John interrupted him then studied the young man, "and Stephanie," he had noticed her discomfort at conflicting with Mark. "I understand this might make you uncomfortable, but I've learned that sometimes you go with who's right for the job and not who's senior. I once started a high visibility, extensive investigation. My firm had been retained to investigate a variety of issues at a high-profile public company. I had been the lead person with the contact at the law firm who brought us into the matter. The lead attorney was a seasoned partner who was highly regarded, and we seemed to click, and he connected with me immediately. We had an initial kick-off meeting with all the relevant stakeholders, including the company executives in a large conference room. Our law firm client had four or five people, and we had me and several of the senior partners from my firm. As the meeting was about to begin and seats were being selected around the table, the lead partner at the law firm sat down. I motioned for my boss, a more experienced partner, to sit down next to him. The lead partner seeing me do this, said to me, 'No, I want you to sit here.' So, while it was temporarily awkward, I took the place of my boss and sat next to the client's senior leader. My boss sat in a chair next to me on my other side.

"During the meeting, another one of my firm colleagues, again a senior partner, commented on some of the issues raised and seemed to have a definitive opinion about them. He came across as an expert even though we were very much at the start of the investigation. I thought his words were generally relevant to the topic, but we—my firm— had not learned enough of the details to go deeper—be so specific—as he had done. His comments kind of hung in the air after they were said, and I thought no one else had picked up on them. After some further discussion, we took a short recess and then reconvene. As I was about to stand from my chair, another law firm partner for our client, whom I knew pretty well, walked by and leaned over and whispered in my ear, 'I don't care what you have to do, but your partner—the one who shared his opinions—has got to go and not return to the table.' I sat slightly stunned for a moment and realized I would have to let that person— senior to me—know they were not wanted back at the table. I felt uncomfortable having to pass on this message, but it was what the client had requested, so it needed to be done. I talked to my colleague in the most sensitive way I could and passed on that they did not want him to return to the table. While these situations are awkward, the requests of the client come first despite any internal planning on who is expected to lead an engagement regardless of title or years of experience. I successfully drove the engagement and earned a 'battlefield' promotion along the way.

"So, Mark, when I saw that the client responded more to Stephanie, that decided for me. There will be times when the client prefers you, and you'll have opportunities to lead the engagement team."

THE IMPORTANCE OF BEING STRAIGHTFORWARD

"Mark, we talked about this once before."

"Did Stephanie complain?" An irritated look spread over Mark's face.

"Sit down, Mark." John pointed at the chair in front of his desk. "The client's CEO mentioned it at the industry event I was at last night. I've worked with her before, and she knew it'd be a good idea I talked with you. I asked Stephanie about it first since she was in earlier than you, and she was right to pull you to the side at the meeting and suggest sticking specifically to what we know and can do well. This is an important lesson I learned back when I was not yet a partner-level professional. My firm was asked to submit a proposal to support the work of a government-mandated monitor for a company that had settled a matter with the federal government. I didn't know the attorneys that had been retained to be the monitor. I also learned that we—my firm—did not know any of the attorneys, and they knew nothing about us—so there weren't any friendly faces. The lead partner was a seasoned practitioner who had decades of experience. She asked me to meet with them at the law firm and go over our proposal. At the time, I had not had this exact experience of supporting a monitor in carrying out their various mandates. However, I had experience with the issues involved. In the meeting with the partner, she asked a series of probing questions, and I did the best I could to answer them to her satisfaction. I was clear I hadn't performed this type of engagement before, but I was familiar with the issues involved. And I described how my prior experience as an auditor was very similar to the required tasks of this engagement. I could sense her skepticism and that she was on the fence about hiring us. I left the meeting, not knowing which way things would go. She hired us, and I think it was because my answers to her about the specific experiences I had and my technical expertise were transparent. I could successfully highlight how we could help her in her role, and that outweighed the fact I had not performed this type of engagement. There is always a first time for everything, and sometimes an informed client will take the leap of faith to hire you as they believe in you."

Why 'Overworking' A Client Is Not A Good Thing

"Have you heard the phrase, too much of a good thing?" John saw their eyes flicker toward each other.

"Sure... my dad used to say that." Stephanie nodded.

"Yes, but for me, it was from my mother," Mark replied.

"So, you know what it means then." John leaned back in his chair and studied the two junior executives. "Do you think it's good to deliver more to the client than you should just to impress them?" He noticed Stephanie squirm in her chair.

"Doesn't it, though? Impress them, I mean...." Mark replied.

"It can but not if the client's not on board with the extra effort. I once worked with a practitioner who spent many hours on an assignment without keeping the client informed of the status and extent of the work being performed. They justified the additional effort by thinking, 'the client will be blown away by all the value we added here.' Well, the client was blown away... not by the value-added but by the size of the fees on the invoice. The client told us: 'You guys really know how to bill,' which is the last thing you want a client to say about you. Thankfully we course-corrected and did not lose that one. But done again or in other circumstances, it might be the last time you hear from that client."

* * *

-------- Original Message --------
Subject: the importance of listening to
what's said and not said - from my journal
notes of what you taught me
From: "Sophia Omondi"
Date: May 1
To: "John"

John,

I thought about this last night. With this
NGO, I've had to do a lot of listening and
learning. Though born here—in Kenya—I left it
when very young, and there's so much to learn
and comprehend to do things right. It starts—
just like what you taught me about clients—
with understanding what's needed. Here are my
notes you can share with Mark and Stephanie:

LISTEN TO WHAT YOUR CLIENT SAYS

When you have the opportunity of having
a client reach out to you, it is vital to
listen carefully to what they are expressing.
Sometimes the need is evident, and they are
looking for an expert with experience with
A, B, and C. Other times, they are trying to
determine themselves what type of resources
they need to address an issue. It is essential
to listen carefully and keep an open mind
and open ears and not start to automatically
categorize what they are describing in terms
of any preconceived notions you may have.

In a client meeting, you may hear them say
that they are looking for help with three
issues. They outline each one in order. After

they are finished, I would ask which one do they think is the highest priority and which one needs to be completed first. I would typically go back over each issue as they described it and articulate it back to them using additional wording to flesh out what they are looking for. In this dialog of going back and forth, the client may realize that there are additional considerations they had not thought of. In this discussion, it will provide the opportunity for you to highlight relevant experiences you or your firm has had and how it was resolved.

Assess What They Really Need

"I know you think you understand what you thought I said, but I'm not sure you realize that what you heard is not what I meant." - Robert McCloskey

Once a client has described their request, it is an excellent practice to echo back to them your understanding of their needs. This is an effective way to avoid initial misunderstandings about what the client is requesting. You may phrase the response in saying, "so you are looking for someone who has deep expertise in this aspect of an industry, is that correct?". By having a back-and-forth discussion with the client, you can help to clarify the need and sometimes help the client refine what they are looking for. In some ways, you are akin to a medical doctor listening to a patient's symptoms, so you want to make sure you have as much accurate information as possible, so you can be able to prescribe the best treatment for the ailment.

CONSIDER OTHER AREAS THEY HAVE NOT MENTIONED

A client may be so focused on one aspect of a matter, that they have not considered some other resources that may be helpful to their efforts. It can be beneficial to the client to raise additional services that may be relevant to more efficiently address their issues. The acquisition and analysis of large amounts of electronic data is typically a need in many cases, so it may be helpful to inquire whether or how they are addressing this aspect. The need for foreign language skills is another area that is sometimes overlooked initially depending on whether there is a global aspect to the matter. The ability required here as a practitioner is to really think about what additional specific services may be needed on a particular subject and not just mention a litany of the services your firm may offer. You do not want to come across like you are trying to maximize your fees instead of trying to be a helpful partner in taking on this new task.

* * *

-------- Original Message --------
Subject: RE: something you learned well that I met with Stephanie and Mark on today
From: "Sophia Omondi"
Date: May 9
To: "John"

John,

Today I talked with one of our primary backers for the NGO and something I said—

about treating an organization's money as if it was my own and tied to a budget and prudent spending—resonated with them. It made me recall something you told me early in my career, and I found it in my journals. Here it is:

ACT AS IF YOU WERE PAYING THE BILLS

Sell to their needs—not from yours. -Earl G. Graves, Sr.

As a professional service provider, you presumably bring a level of expertise and experience that is not commonly available. Therefore, the value you bring should bear a billing rate commensurate with that level. Though this comes into play more at senior executive levels and management determination of pricing for engagements, even when a junior (or even new) executive or associate, you must have an awareness of your hourly billing rate and a project's estimated cost. Because that is what the client will be reviewing and ultimately paying. Just like you would ask a house painter for an estimate to paint all or some part of your home, it is helpful for you to put yourself in the shoes of the buyer of your professional services and to be able to explain the elements of the proposed fees. Your client is trusting in you to be fair in your estimate of fees. So any efforts you make to increase efficiencies and minimize costs will be appreciated. This does not mean that you artificially low ball the fees on an assignment but instead to again put yourself in the shoes of the client, so you can understand and articulate why these fees are required.

POINTS TO THINK ABOUT

Take a moment and reflect on what you've read and consider:

1. The last time you were with a potential client, how much were you talking vs. how much were you listening?

2. Do you clarify and confirm with the potential client what services they are looking for?

3. How often do you try to put yourself in the shoes of the client and expect what they may ask or say?

CHAPTER 3 – ESTABLISHING TRUST & DELIVERING ON IT

If people like you they'll listen to you, but if they trust you, they'll do business with you.

—Zig Ziglar

THE NEW OFFICE
THE IMPORTANCE OF CREATING SINCERE CONNECTIONS

"**Y**ou've both seen some of the practical sides of this business now. And I hope you've listened to my advice and examples from my experience. It's how I've learned as I built my career and this company, before selling it to Sophia." John half-turned in his chair to point a thumb at the sign over his desk. "Do that, and I know you'll find success too."

"Helping isn't selling, but it leads to sales?" Stephanie asked.

"Right. But it also leads to what's more important. Connecting."

"When we sell... I mean help a client and do the work... that's connecting, isn't it?" Mark's fingers tapped the arm of his chair. "No connection means no sale." The fingers stopped.

"You're thinking transactional, Mark, and that's part of it. But developing a connection goes much deeper."

"That sounds like doing more than was needed or required, and you told us not to 'overwork' a client." Mark's finger drum roll began again.

"It's a big-picture perspective, Mark. A 'give a man a fish, feed him for a day. Teach a man to fish, and he can feed himself for a lifetime,' philosophy."

"As long as there's fish to catch...." Stephanie said.

Mark gave her a surprised glance. "That's right--"

John nodded, "You're both right. I'll back up a bit to be clear about that metaphor. It's the principle, the mechanism within it, and not the 'fish' that's important to understand. The point I want to make with it is the process of developing long-lasting connections. Being known as helpful and sincere is what creates an environment of opportunity to help others, or those they know and can refer to you, who can use your services. While I was managing a large project a few years ago, my colleagues were working in close tandem for many months with a team of attorneys from a law firm. Throughout the engagement, one of my closest friends from my firm and a good friend from the law firm began working together and learned of each other's interest in firearms and history. They were both very passionate about hunting. Sorry, it wasn't fishing," John smiled and continued. "Eventually, they started going on annual outings and over the years, have become close friends who continue to hunt and spend time with each other's family. You never know where the sharing of common interests may take you and your relationship with a client."

"Another colleague and I who appreciate wine and have been involved in the wine industry and as a collector, attended a law firm-sponsored event where they served several very nice wines. We knew one attorney and started talking about the wine. We soon learned he was quite the aficionado and also a collector. He mentioned that another attorney at a different firm who was at the event was also a wine buff. We all four talked about some of our wine experiences and connected on the topic. I suggested a wine tasting dinner for the four of us where we would each bring a bottle (or two) of some of our collection of wines we enjoyed. We could do the tasting at a local restaurant that had a low corkage fee. We ended up having the dinner and tried many superb wines and delicious food. We also learned about each other and our families and created a bond. We have since had a recurring wine tasting dinner once or twice a year, and our relationships have deepened. Those attorneys have reached out to me with potential opportunities, and they have provided strong recommendations to others looking for help on a matter I have experience and expertise in. So, you never know where the road you've built can take you or what it will lead to... just know that it can be to opportunities."

WHY MONITORING—FOLLOWING UP— ON A REFERRAL IS CRITICAL

"John, do you have a couple of minutes?" Mark said from the office doorway.

"Sure." John set aside the folder he had been reviewing.

"What's up?"

"I have a client that needs something done, but it's not in my area of expertise. I think with help, I could do it, but I thought about what you said about focusing on what I know I can do, but if they need something other than that to refer them to someone with the right skillset and experience. And I think that's Bob Henderson. But this is a good client, and I'm worried about handing them off. Any tips on best practices?" Mark grinned, "C'mon... I know you have some."

John laughed and nodded. "When referring a colleague to one of your clients, it's important to stay engaged in the discussions and not just do a simple hand-off without further involvement. I once was contacted by a client looking for a specific skill set that someone else in my firm possessed. I put the client and my colleague together, stepped back, and did not take part further in any discussions. Some time passed, and I talked with the client again and inquired about the opportunity she referred. The client said that they had one phone call and that nothing further came. My colleague never followed up, and an opportunity was missed. When you refer a client to a colleague, stay involved in the conversation to ensure that the client is receiving the proper attention, and finding the right resources. How your referred colleague treats the client may be a reflection upon you and how the client views you. Reputational management is important, so don't think whoever you referred has your back. Make sure. Bob's a good man, so you should be okay. But still do your follow-up."

Mentoring Session – The Cost Of Feeling Something's Not Worth The Time

"Have either of you read *The Tipping Point* by Malcolm Gladwell?"

"It is about how some things go big, they tip to success... and some don't." Stephanie replied.

"Right," Mark nodded, "and that it seems to happen suddenly."

"But that there are underlying reasons, some quite small, that add up over time—sometimes a lengthy period—that 'tip' things. I'm glad you both read it because I want to stress how important little things, sometimes things you don't think worthwhile, make a difference in the long run. A past colleague of mine had a family friend who worked as a general counsel of a large company. At an outing, she inquired of my colleague if his firm provided certain services. My colleague put his family friend in touch with a colleague who had specific expertise. My colleague did not follow-up with his friend after the introduction as he felt like he did not want her to feel like he was pressuring her or making their relationship just about business. Eventually, they met again at a social outing, and the general counsel let him know they would not need the services. So, an opportunity was lost, potentially because of the lack of follow-up. Understand that while there is a balance between maintaining a friendship and providing services to a family friend, the friend was seeking help, and my then- colleague was able to help her and did not. One way to view this is that when a friend asks for help, you're going to try to help them, and providing services is just another way to help them even though it is business-oriented."

Mentoring Session – Selling Yourself First And Not Over-Selling The Company

"Uh oh," Mark tapped Stephanie's shoulder, "Looks like more whiteboard talk..."

"Grab some coffee and sit." John waited until they were at the conference room table. "Okay, I've talked a lot that helping not selling is how you develop new and recurring clients." He picked up a dry-erase marker. "Now I'm going to talk about selling," he noted their expression. "I knew you'd enjoy the topic, Mark... and Stephanie, that you'd be a bit concerned." John turned to write on the board. "Here's the order—the sequence—you must follow, a seasoned sales executive gave me this advice about selling. That before a client will hire you, you need to...." He wrote:

1. Sell Yourself

2. Sell your Company

3. Sell your Product/Service

"I think the most important—where everything else starts—is the first step: Accomplish it by being yourself. Be confident and look to help them. Show that you have taken the time to understand their business. Second: Selling your company is knowing what your firm provides can help them and being knowledgeable about the resources you can call upon is essential in determining that. It's a critical part of presenting the solution they need. Selling your product/service is best done when you've listened to your client to understand accurately what that need is and what they are looking for in a solution provider. Be honest and transparent in your offering of how you and your firm can meet their needs. The underlying premise for#2 and #3 is the same," he smiled at Mark, "I wasn't teasing you about making an emphasis on selling yourself. The best way to do that is by showing how your company, your product, or service helps the client. You do that by listening and asking good questions. And that process—showing a smart approach—of a true professional, sells the client on you... your capabilities and that of the firm you represent."

DON'T COMPROMISE CLIENT RELATIONSHIPS BY 'CHASING' THE NEXT NEW CLIENT

John waited for Mark to return from walking the client out. He waved him into his office. "Let's talk about how accountability and responsibility pay off and that it's what gets you follow-on business and new referrals. Through a connection I had at a law firm, we were invited to present our qualifications for a significant international investigation related to a global company. We had already submitted our written proposal with our team and approach, and the senior partner asked me to meet with him and the client as a next step in the retention process. I went to the law firm's offices and was told that the team and the client were in a meeting and I should wait in a conference room. After a while, the senior partner came in, and he was a pretty intense, focused professional. He came in and said he had read the proposal, and it seemed we had good resources to do the work and noted I was positioned to lead the overall engagement. He sat relatively close to me and told me: 'The client, and we will be heavily relying on you to get this job done. You'll be critical to the success of this, and there is no room for mistakes.' He was looking directly at me and speaking increasingly louder. 'I need to know that you will be committed to this and to know that we will all depend on you to perform successfully. Will you be able to do that? Are you committed to doing this?' I could feel the importance he placed on this role and sensed he was testing me to see how I would respond. If I blinked or coughed and responded in a less than satisfying way, I was pretty sure he would not hire me for the project. I was confident in myself and the team we had assembled for this matter, and I told him: 'My team and I are absolutely committed to this, and I appreciate the importance of getting it right. I will do whatever it takes to make sure we are meeting yours and the client's needs.' He listened to me and seemed to accept my response, but once again emphasized the trust he placed in me. He then went to introduce me to the client which was a cordial and brief meeting without really any vetting of us by the client. I think once the senior partner understood and believed I was committed to the successful completion of the engagement, he relaxed, and we went about planning the engagement. We were retained, and the success of that project led to several others."

"Okay, I get that... thanks." Mark started to turn to leave.

"Mark, my point in telling you that is because, in the meeting, we just finished, you started to—seemed like—

you lost focus."

"I've got that RFP on another company to reply to today." Mark's feet shifted toward the door.

"Hang on a second... I know that new business-chasing and catching a new client can be exciting. It gets you all pumped up. We all enjoy the thrill of bringing in new business. But think about this: don't lose sight of what you do—or will do—for the clients you already have. They're the ones that can help you land new business for years to come."

* * *

```
-------- Original Message --------
Subject: the importance of not being just
transactional - from my journal notes of
what you taught me
From: "Sophia Omondi"
Date: June 1
To: "John"
```

John,

What you told me about your last session with Mark and Stephanie is precisely one of the lessons most critical to success. And when you first explained it to me... it made me feel better. I was much like Stephanie but had some of Mark's aggressive edge. What you taught me brought the two positive perspectives together into one. I went back and read in my journals some of the things I noted that have helped me avoid treating clients—or prospective new clients—as just 'transactions.' Please share with Mark and Stephanie:

ENGAGE CLIENTS ON PERSONAL ISSUES

Getting to know a client beyond a professional capacity can deepen your relationship with them and helps give them a better sense of who you are as a person. You may find that some clients have little or no interest in getting to know you outside of the professional relationship. They may just be looking for help and don't have the time, energy, or interest in going into personal discussions. However, you will not know until you try, so I suggest always being yourself but also attempt to learn more about the client and their life situation. Being friendly to others and exhibiting a sense of humor are outstanding traits to possess generally, and you may find that some clients will be open to a more casual conversation and respond in-kind.

1. Consider sports, theater, kid's events, travel stories
2. Find something you both share in common

DISCUSS OUTSIDE INTERESTS AND HOBBIES

The more that you learn about a client, the more you may come to realize that you share some common interests. Alternatively, you may discover that you do not really share any common interest and conceivably could have conflicting interests, so it is essential to share this information thoughtfully with no judgments or strong opposition that could be considered offensive or a turnoff. You may find that you share an interest in classic cars, social issues, sports, wine tasting, and many other areas of potential joint interest.

POINTS TO THINK ABOUT

Take a moment and reflect on what you've read and consider:

1. When was the last time you engaged with a client on non-business issues?
2. How often do you see a client outside of the specific engagement you worked on together?
3. Do you understand what outside interests your clients have?

CHAPTER 4 – CONNECTING THROUGH SOCIALIZATION

The difference between Selling and Helping is just two letters.

–Jay Baer

AT THE INDUSTRY CONFERENCE
THE BALANCE BETWEEN BEING 'TOO PASSIVE' AND 'TOO AGGRESSIVE'

"Well, what do you think about your first major industry expo and conference?" John caught the eye of the waiter. "More coffee, please, and two more cups, this lady and gentleman are joining me."

Mark pulled a chair out and sat. "It's great... so many C-suite level people to talk to."

"It's fine, it seems a good way to make contacts." Stephanie took the cup the waiter set before her and filled it with coffee from the fresh carafe.

John took the carafe, topped off his cup, and handed the decanter to Mark. Taking two sips, he studied the young junior executives. "Both of you should think about what we've talked about. What works in meetings and conference rooms back home, works here too. And you both—I say this after watching you last evening—are out of balance."

"What do you mean by 'balance'?" Stephanie asked. Mark nodded; he had the same question as he bit into a croissant.

"Did you notice how people 'wandered' away from you after that first bit of introduction and conversation?"

Both nodded. Mark commented. "Isn't that—talking to as many people as possible—what you're supposed to do at these things? I mean, meet as many as possible and keep moving."

"That's part of it, but you want meaningful—two-way—conversations. When they bail out quickly, people you just met seem to find a reason to stop talking with you... that's usually a sign you're too focused on selling," John eyed Mark then shifted to Stephanie. "Or not at all. I want both of you to understand that events like the one last night are valuable opportunities. Still, you must approach them in the right way, and you can often set the stage yourself. You find your balance by listening to needs or potential needs and engagingly presenting your thoughts in a non-sales environment. Like one year at a conference in New York City. I suggested to the attorney who was the program leader that our firm host a simple happy hour the night before the conference, so some of the attendees who were local to New York and those coming in from out of town could meet and mingle. We arranged to have a portion of the restaurant bar of a hotel near the conference set aside for our cocktail party. We had several clients attend and some new folks.

"I introduced the program leader to one of my New York colleagues during the event, and they had a very engaging discussion. Several months went by, and then I was contacted to assist with a proposal request that came from the attorney who served as the conference program leader to my colleague whom he had met at our reception. We were able to propose on the opportunity and won the engagement. On another occasion, a colleague invited a client to a Bruce Springsteen concert in a corporate suite. Several clients were attending, and between the food and drink and the Boss's performance, it was a delightful and memorable evening. The client contacted my colleague the next day about a new opportunity. We proposed on and won the work, which turned out to be a multi-million-dollar engagement. Still another time, I set up a lunch with a client who I had worked with in the past. It was in a steak restaurant and very relaxed. We talked about how our kids were doing and the vacations we had taken. We didn't talk about work and business until after halfway through the meal. I inquired what she had been working on, and she said she had a big case starting in China that would require gathering a lot of electronic data from systems and laptops of employees. I told her we had an office in Hong Kong that did that work. 'Good to know!' she told me, 'I need to submit proposals for vendors to the client.' Not long after that dinner, she requested I submit a proposal with the requisite experience. We ended up being hired for the engagement.

"We can build trust through shared social experiences that don't involve constant 'pitching' to the client. Clients and prospects learn about their firm's capabilities via social interaction and indirect discussion. And that can absolutely lead to sales."

* * *

```
-------- Original Message --------
Subject: practicing inclusivity is a good
business practice - from my journal notes of
what you taught me
From: "Sophia Omondi"
Date: July 6
To: "John"
```

John,

I'm multicultural—born in Kenya, raised and educated in England, professional career and adult life in America—and for that true meaning to strike me took coming back to Kenya. Stepping away, with the luxury of shifting my focus thanks to you, has made me realize how vital inclusivity is to understanding people. And that means clients too. To become inclusive means reaching out because it will never happen without action, and its benefits never develop in a vacuum. Like I mentioned in reply to one of your recent lessons for Mark, new business and client development do not have to be transactional. It's wise to include clients and client prospects without immediate quid pro quo. Take a 'no strings attached' approach and make the setting comfortable. When people—even clients and prospects—are in a relaxed environment, you can form connections that last long term. Here are some of my notes and thoughts on that for Mark and Stephanie:

Invite Clients And Prospective Clients To Sponsored Events

Another way of helping potential clients is to include them and invite them to business and community events. An excellent way to improve your relationship with a contact is to ask them to present on a firm-sponsored program or conference. These days, these events may take the form of a webcast where a specific subject and timely issue may be discussed with a panel of experienced professionals. This is an excellent forum for your contact to highlight their depth of knowledge in a subject area and can also serve for them to appreciate your knowledge and experience. While many of these presentations on conference panels and webcasts may only run for an hour or so, the time spent with the contact planning for and executing the talk serves to further grow the understanding and trust between you and the contact. These platforms also help to give yourself and your connection additional exposure to potential clients who are in attendance or listen to the webcast. There is a myriad of events where you can think to include your contacts, and they typically appreciate the invitation, which can generate additional goodwill toward you.

Get Tickets To A Game Or A Show

An excellent way to get to know a client and have some fun is to invite the client to a sporting event or concert. In some firms, they may subscribe to season tickets for the local sports team, which are intended to be used as a client development opportunity. Depending on your position in the firm, you may be offered access to the sporting events. Even if you are not provided access, there will probably be available tickets, and you may reserve them if you express an interest and have a client or potential client to invite. Or you may purchase your own tickets to an event and receive a reimbursement for the cost from the firm.

While a new engagement may not result from taking your client to one event, it will allow you to spend time with a client in a more relaxed environment where you can bond outside of the work environment. A client may be very appreciative, especially when you can include an invitation to the client and their family members, as they may already have limited time with their family, and this provides them with time together.

TAKE THEM TO LUNCH OR MEET FOR COFFEE/DRINKS

Treating a client to lunch or grabbing a coffee or cocktail is an excellent way to continue to catch up and to stay top of mind. I have found that many clients have limited time for a meal or drink, and you may need to try several times to find a mutually workable date to get together.

POINTS TO THINK ABOUT

Take a moment and reflect on what you've read and consider:

1. When was the last time you invited a client out to an event?

2. Are you aware of events at your firm where you could invite clients?

3. What was the last event you attended with a client?

4. How often do you stay in touch with the clients you have worked with?

CHAPTER 5 –
MAINTAIN CONTACT
WITH CLIENTS

*The glue that holds all relationships together...
is trust, and trust is based on integrity.*
                                    –Brian Tracy

THE NEW OFFICE
How To Keep Your Firm In Colleagues', Clients' (Or Prospects') Minds

John settled back in his chair and half-turned to glance at the photo—the one of his old office sign—Sophia had put on the wall behind his desk. He cocked his thumb at it and turned back to Stephanie and Mark: "CSIH. One way to keep in contact with clients to help—not sell—them is to share news and articles that are relevant and have some value to them. And that is an excellent way to touch base with them. I often come across these items and share them. I once shared an article about a possible improper type of corporate behavior in a specific industry with an attorney who represented clients in that industry. After a back-and-forth discussion with the attorney, they indicated they would reach out to their clients to get an assessment of the possibility of this behavior occurring in

JAMES W. BARRATT

their companies. After receiving feedback from them with mixed results, the attorney came back and said that at least one of their clients had a potential concern and had kept them for testing be performed. The attorney hired us—in part since I had sent them the article—as the consultant to assist them in the work.

"Another time, I was aware of an upcoming conference that would be of interest to a group of attorneys who practiced in a particular subject area. I sent a group email notice informing them about the event and received several email responses back, thanking me. Doing things like that keeps you top of mind to some attorneys. One attorney, who was a senior partner I had worked with in the past, sent one of the thank you responses. I replied to his email and said that I hoped all was well and to inform them I was just finishing up a couple of matters, and to please keep me in mind for any projects I could provide some help. The attorney quickly responded that they may need our services on a matter shortly. And a month later, he contacted me with an opportunity that led to a new engagement."

Two Weeks Later

"Hey John, guess what?"

John had to smile when he saw the huge grin on Stephanie's face as she came down the hall toward him. "What?"

"It worked!"

"What worked?"

"I sent a really good article to a client. They passed it

on, and I got a new client!"

* * *

```
-------- Original Message --------
Subject: One of the most important lessons I
learned from you - from my journal notes of
what you taught me
From: "Sophia Omondi"
Date: August 12
To: "John"
```

John,

That's great news about Stephanie using what you told her and Mark, and that she got a new client from it! You might have already gone over this with Mark and Stephanie—I know how important you feel it is—but here are my journal notes from one of the most important lessons you taught me:

FIND WAYS TO STAY IN CONTACT
AFTER AN ENGAGEMENT

Probably the best way to develop and maintain a strong client relationship is to work with them on an assignment where there is constant interaction, discussions, and challenging but successful outcomes. The experience of working closely with a client for extended periods in sometimes difficult circumstances may be akin to being teammates on a sports team or going to battle against a common adversary where you are committed to each other and to the mission. While an incredibly powerful bond can develop on shared assignments, eventually, the project comes to an end, and you will go your separate ways. The nature of consulting work is that you will then be off to another project with new clients, and your attention is redirected. What can be vitally important but sometimes very challenging is to maintain the level of collegiality and familiarity that you shared with the client when you were knee deep in the throes of your joint project. While you may have moved on with your new day-to-day routine, it is essential to find ways to maintain and build on the relationship you developed with the client. Remaining top of mind with your clients is one of the most critical parts of keeping your client relationship healthy and increases the potential for recurring work with the client. There are a variety of actions you can take to preserve and build the post-engagement relationship, and they require constant vigilance and discipline. We all may fall into a bit of laziness when it comes to staying in touch with our former clients. Still, just like being a friend, be there for the client whether or not you are working on a project together.

-------- Original Message --------
Subject: RE: One of the most important lessons I learned from you - from my journal notes of what you taught me
From: "John"
Date: August 27
To: "Sophia Omondi"

Sophia,

I talked with Stephanie and Mark about that today. Also, I shared that when you forward a relevant article or news story to a client, it creates another touchpoint that can help keep you top of mind to them. Thoughtful consideration of what you share and how often is warranted as nobody wants to get yet another email about a subject that they already well know or is irrelevant to their area of focus. When presented correctly, a client will appreciate a timely, useful article as it keeps them up to speed. It also reminds them you know what their interests are and that you are considerate in sharing it with them.

I told Stephanie and Mark that sharing an article or your take on the implications of the subject of the article then triggers a dialog between yourself and your client and is another good outcome that may lead to potential work. I also discussed the following:

SEND AN OCCASIONAL EMAIL JUST TO CHECK-IN

Sometimes it is a friendly gesture to send a message to a client only to see how they are doing and how work is going. Authenticity and not seeking or asking for potential work can help to develop a level of respect and friendship that can be well received and further strengthen your connection with a client.

Modestly priced gifts of appreciation can be an excellent way to stay in touch with clients. At one firm I worked at, the firm would send a box of tasty brownies to select clients. The brownies were typically shared with the client's colleagues, and they were very appreciative. It was such a popular gift that clients would look forward to them each Thanksgiving, and it raised the awareness of the firm and generated thoughtful responses from the client.

Keep Clients (And Prospects) Updated On Your Firm's Activities

As additional personnel and resources are added to your firm, it is useful to share the news with your clients and contacts. One firm I worked for acquired a practice that included international offices. It was good for clients to be aware there were now capabilities in Europe, Asia, and the Middle East.

In another case, an individual with specialized expertise related to data privacy joined the firm. The new employee's announcement of joining the firm, along with a description of the type of matters they had worked on, was sent around to a variety of clients. One client was very interested in the skill set as they had an issue where they needed an expert. It connected the new employee with the client. After a robust discussion and an in-person meeting, they were retained as an expert. It is hard to predict what all of your clients may be working on at a particular point in time, so it is worth sharing information about new professionals, additional skillsets, and expanded geographic locations.

POINTS TO THINK ABOUT

Take a moment and reflect on what you've read and consider:

1. What do you do to maintain contact with clients?

2. How often do you reach out to your clients?

3. Have you sent a client an article or news story in the last month?

CHAPTER 6 –
SPEND MORE TIME ON
EXISTING CLIENTS

If you can dream it, then you can achieve it. You will get all you want in life if you help enough other people get what they want.

–Zig Ziglar

THE NEW OFFICE
LEVERAGING LARGE CLIENT RELATIONSHIPS FOR BUSINESS DEVELOPMENT

"The client loved our work; the end of the project meeting went great." Mark leaned back, hands behind his head.

"Congratulations, well done!" John sat down across from him.

"Stephanie and I were talking on the drive from the airport." Mark lowered his arms and rolled his chair closer to the table. "This client has a dozen divisions. How can we use what we've done and explore getting in with them too?"

"That's excellent thinking, Mark. A supportive client within a larger firm with multiple service lines can provide you with a springboard to meet and work with additional colleagues of the client. A friendly, satisfied client will sometimes invite you to meet more of their colleagues. This invitation can create the opportunity for you to meet potential clients in your area of expertise and the chance to educate them about other services your firm provides. A warm introduction from a trusted colleague is one of the easiest and most effective ways to meet new potential clients. It can give you an immediate 'seal of approval' that otherwise may require a significant amount of time and effort on your behalf to achieve. Besides a friendly invitation from an existing client, depending on the depth of your relationship, you may want to ask the client who else in their firm would be right for you to meet. This inquiry puts the onus on the client to think about which of their colleagues could benefit from meeting you, however, they may identify colleagues who you were not familiar with. Another approach is to ask the existing client to make an introduction to specific colleagues of theirs that you may have already researched and identified or have otherwise had a difficult time getting to meet. If done correctly, this direct ask will not come across as too aggressive or manipulative. Give that a shot and let me know if you need any help."

WHAT IF A CLIENT WANTS 'IN-HOUSE' HELP?

"Hey John, did you ever have a client ask about hiring you to work at their company?"

Mark looked up from the client folder he had just opened on John's desk and shot a puzzled look at Stephanie sitting next to him. "You mean one of yours offered you a job?"

"Not exactly, but they need someone with my skills to fill a management position temporarily. And, well, they like me too."

John leaned back in his chair and steepled his fingers, "I have had something like that happen, Stephanie. Our firm was already assisting a client with a separate set of tasks, and they also required a compliance officer. They needed someone in the position as soon as possible as they wanted to develop and stand up a robust compliance program. I was put forward as a candidate to serve as the interim compliance officer, given some of my background experience. I had provided my biography and had a phone call with my colleague, who was already working at the company and one of the people relevant to the project. The company wanted to meet with me, so I flew to their office on the West Coast, where I met several of the members of local senior management and then met with the head of Human Resources. In that meeting, I sat across the desk from her as she reviewed my biography and asked questions. I told her about my similar experience in the area of expertise they needed, and she inquired what my approach was on that matter. The conversation then shifted to the issues at the company, and I asked her questions so I could learn more. Our conversation helped define what they were looking for in that specific role. I had started the discussion providing my thoughts and feedback based on the limited understanding I had, but as I learned more asking questions and listening to her answers, the dynamic of the conversation switched from a candidate interview to more of a colleague brainstorming session where specific steps to be performed were developed. By the end of the meeting, she was clearly enthusiastic about me assisting them. I was retained to help the company in establishing a compliance function and worked well as an interim part of the management team. It allowed my firm to show trustworthiness—through me—for future engagements."

* * *

-------- Original Message --------
Subject: current clients are your best resource - from my journal notes of what you taught me
From: "Sophia Omondi"
Date: September 1
To: "John"

John,

That's excellent news that Stephanie has a client interested in utilizing her skills and capabilities to fill a short-term need within their company. I think that's a testimonial to what they are learning, some of which we've touched on in our email correspondence. Listen to clients, understand their needs, and how your capabilities can fulfill them, and treat the client as more than a transaction. That approach pays off. Please add my following thoughts to your talks with Stephanie and Mark:

EXISTING CLIENTS WHO LIKE YOU ARE THE BEST SOURCE OF BUSINESS

Have you ever experienced the feeling of satisfaction you get when you find a product that works just as you want it to or a professional who helps you deal with a challenging issue and resolves it successfully? That level of satisfaction is what professionals always strive for with their clients. There is a phrase, "happy spouse, happy house," and in business, a comparable expression could be "happy client, happy business." One of the best sources of repeat business is a happy client. When you have worked with a client and achieved a significant outcome on a project, they are typically very grateful. While this can make the payment of your fees easier, it also serves as a valuable point of reference about you and the quality of the services provided. These happy clients are more likely to look for opportunities to work together with you again and will usually be glad to refer you to other colleagues in their firm or even friendly competitors at other firms. Since you have already developed a strong reputation with this client, it can pay dividends to you in the future. Once you have a client as a big fan, you need to maintain and nurture that relationship. You have likely already invested your blood, sweat, and tears in reaching a great outcome, so it is essential to retain and further develop this goodwill.

DO NOT TAKE THE RELATIONSHIP FOR GRANTED – BE A FRIEND

-------- Original Message --------
Subject: RE: current clients are your best resource - from my journal notes of what you taught me
From: "John"
Date: September 2
To: "Sophia Omondi"

Sophia,

I'll add your notes/thoughts in your previous email to my next talk with Stephanie and Mark (who is starting to show he is listening to and learning from us).

Something that complements your last email's notes is: Don't forget, once you have developed a great relationship with a client and they are one of your ardent supporters, you mustn't take the relationship for granted and assume that they are always thinking about you. After the time and effort, you have put into developing a strong client relationship, it only makes sense to continue to ensure that the connection remains alive and well. You can sometimes be lulled into a sense of false comfort that your client is only dedicated to you and would not think about reaching out to a competitor. Just like the old saying by Ralph Waldo Emerson goes, "the only way to have a friend is to be one," a successful, lasting relationship with a client is a function of what you put into it. Reach out to a client and just say hello and see how they are doing. If you come across something that could be of value to them and their business, such as an article or conference, bring it to their attention to show that you are thinking about them. While it may seem like a pretty simple activity to stay in touch with clients and maintain the relationship, it becomes more challenging and requires increased dedication as you develop more client relationships. However, when you enjoy helping your clients to succeed, then taking time to maintain the connection can be a positive and upbeat activity for you.

Look For Avenues To Introduce Them To Potential Clients

From time to time, there may be occasions for you to introduce existing clients to potential clients for their business. You may have folks in your network who could utilize your client's services, and an introduction of the two parties could result in a win-win-win for all of you. When you successfully connect the dots between contacts you have developed good relationships with and they find value in the meeting, you have helped them further develop potential business and expanded their individual networks of contacts. Many times, when I have arranged meetings between several contacts, they will inevitably find mutual connections through their discussions, which only serves to further develop a stronger relationship in a timelier way and help make them feel more comfortable with each other.

When Possible, Help Clients With Their Business

It is literally true that you can succeed best and quickest by helping others to succeed. - Napoleon Hill

Find ways to partner with an existing client to highlight their experience and skillsets. If a client is facing a specific problem you have seen addressed at other clients, a few words of insight and direction may help them work to improve their situation. You should not always look to be retained to provide advice to an existing client when you can give them information that does not require a significant amount of your time. You may have in-depth knowledge about a specific area, and even a few questions about the client's situation, along with some potential items to consider, can go a long way in developing an appreciative client.

POINTS TO THINK ABOUT

Take a moment and reflect on what you've read and consider:

1. What have you done to stay in touch with your best clients?

2. When was the last time you made an introduction to a client of someone who may help their business?

3. Have you provided any "free advice" to a good client recently?

4. When was the last time a good client introduced you to some of their colleagues?

CHAPTER 7 – MAKE NEW CONTACTS

Give me six hours to chop down a tree, and I will spend the first four sharpening the ax.
                                        –Abraham Lincoln

THE NEW OFFICE
SHOULD YOU FOCUS SOLELY ON DIRECT NETWORK CONTACTS OR A BROADER REACH?

"So, we shouldn't focus solely on the business network we have now, but expand it and look wider?"

"Your core network is something you want to refine... that's your 'go-to' bread and butter, Mark. But you want to grow it strategically. As you develop contacts in your careers, you may associate certain contacts with a specific area of work or industry or geography. It's human nature to organize or bucket our contacts. You may have a network of people known through your personal and family life, or through work you perform on community and non-profit efforts. Once I introduced someone from a non-profit which I served on the board, to a client. They shared a common heritage in an African country. They were both interested in improving the quality of life there, much like what Sophia is doing now with her NGO work. While there was not an immediate engagement or potential engagement that came from connecting the contacts, it generated a new enthusiastic connection, and both were grateful to me for introducing them. So, while you may have met someone in a unique situation, it's vital to always think broadly about who else you may know who could be a helpful contact for someone else in your network. As you make more contacts and can serve as a connector of networks, it's more likely people will view you as being a well-connected resource and may seek you out if they are looking for someone with a particular background or expertise."

* * *

```
-------- Original Message --------
Subject: an important part of business I
learned since buying the company from you
From: "Sophia Omondi"
Date: October 4
To: "John"
```

John,

Sorry for the delay in replying. What you told me you told Mark is 'spot on.' Current—happy—clients are an excellent resource for new business. But we have to attend to that client relationship properly, or that does not happen. Done properly, we can leverage that client connection to new business beyond. And that can—should in my belief—mean beyond our domestic border. Mark and Stephanie already know international growth is one of my essential objectives. One I've made some strides in. I want them to explore how they can find and reach global opportunities. Here are my notes and thoughts to share with them: Building trust is critical for global colleagues. As you deal with potential clients around the world, it is crucial to understand the various cultural and personal connections that may differ from U.S. typical behaviors. Having worked in China and other countries, I believe it may be worth trying to work in a scenario to illustrate for Mark and Stephanie. One thought was when I taught a two-day course in China and how different the audience would react or not react to questions that in the U.S., people would likely be more open to answering. But in China, they were concerned about being too outspoken with their views.

* * *

-------- Original Message --------
Subject: RE: an important part of business I learned since buying the company from you
From: "John"
Date: October 5
To: "Sophia Omondi"

Sophia,

When you get back, I'd like to sit in on one of your courses or meetings with global clients. This morning I talked to Stephanie and Mark about what you included in your email and also how to:

MAKE THE WORLD A SMALLER PLACE BY CONNECTING NETWORKS

Some consulting firms are large enough to

hire or have a person in a position as a business developer. Or an individual who is tasked with finding new clients, setting up meetings and developing relationships, and bringing in new business for the professionals within the firm. Many times, these business developers are not subject matter experts but are individuals such as lawyers or other professionals that have backgrounds in the industry and have existing networks or contacts. Or they are a classic salesperson willing to cold-call and do all the things required to establish new connections and make sales. For the professional who is learning client development, a person like that can be helpful if appropriately engaged. One way to enlist their help is to make sure they are aware of your expertise, who your contacts are, and the type of work you have done before. They can then broadcast your capabilities among their contacts and network. So, they have in mind what expertise is available.

It's important to have frequent communication and coordination. Sometimes communication is less than perfect, but it's needed to understand who they are in contact with, so there are no conflicts and to prevent duplicated efforts. Most importantly, it can seem unprofessional or a lack of focus if you talk to one of your contacts, and they tell you, "A person from your firm just called me." At best, you can make light of it, but at worst, it sends a signal of a lack of coordination within your firm.

Not all firms have this type of person, but if they do, they can be used as a benefit. Business developers typically work on a commission-type compensation model and don't provide the actual professional services. Still, they will want to make sure that the engagement goes well so they continue to have potential work from that client.

STRIVE DAILY TO INCREASE YOUR CONTACTS

Your existing and recurring clients may provide you with plenty of work. If you sustain those relationships, it may be possible to achieve a successful business with those clients. However, one should not become complacent and rely only on existing clients as they may retire or move on to other companies, so it is crucial to continue to grow your network of potential clients. It is not enough just to add any new contacts to your network. You should continue to research and identify good potential clients that would likely utilize your services. Also, it is an excellent practice to network with individuals who work in your particular industry who may be able to connect you with good relevant contacts.

POSITION YOURSELF, SO COMPETITORS BECOME A SOURCE FOR REFERRALS

It is good to know who your competitors are in any given field. Understanding the various strengths and weaknesses of each market participant will keep you well informed for your potential clients when they ask questions about how you differ from another provider. Besides being well informed, developing a friendly relationship with your competitors may allow you to both give and receive referrals of work. If a competitor knows you and has an opportunity on which they were approached by a client, but they cannot perform the work for whatever reason, such as a conflict of interest or lack of capacity, they may have the chance to recommend some other providers to their client. Sometimes a client will reach out to you, and you and your firm do not perform that service, but you have a contact that does. By referring to a client someone that you know does a good job, you are helping the client address their issue even though you were not the one performing the work. Also, by referring some work to a friendly competitor, they may return the favor and recommend you and your firm when they have an opportunity that they are not in a position to take the work.

* * *

-------- Original Message --------
Subject: Social Media - this is important in today's market/business environment
From: "Sophia Omondi"
Date: October 19
To: "John"

John,

I know this is not your strong suit, and maybe we can leave the in-depth discussion for when I get back, which is coming soon. But please go over this with Stephanie and Mark:

UTILIZE SOCIAL MEDIA NETWORKS TO INTRODUCE YOURSELF

With social media applications, remember that whatever you may post on Facebook or LinkedIn, for example, could be viewed by a potential client. Depending on the thoroughness of the background check that a potential client may perform on you, your personal posts with family and friends may be reviewed, so you will want to strive to be discreet in what you post. Many professionals utilize LinkedIn to post information about their firm, and themselves and may repost articles of interest or write their own articles to highlight their expertise. Social media networks appropriately used can get your name, face, and biography in front of thousands of people in a short period. Twitter is another application that can make yourself—or your message—known.

POINTS TO THINK ABOUT

Take a moment and reflect on what you've read and consider:

1. What is the size of your network in terms of contacts?

2. How much has your network grown since the same time last year?

3. What steps have you taken in the last three months to increase your network?

4. How do you use social media to expand your contacts?

CHAPTER 8 – MARKETING YOUR SKILLS

It takes 20 years to build a reputation and five minutes to ruin it. If you think about that, you'll do things differently.

—Warren Buffett

THE NEW OFFICE
Your Bio And Cv/Resume Are Important: Keep Them Current

John typed: "Email me your current CV. Don't touch or update it. Send as is without change. Meet me in my office at 10:00 AM tomorrow to discuss why." He pressed send.

Next Morning

John sat behind his desk, the two resumes side by side in front of him. He tapped them as they sat down. "As you gain additional experience on new projects, it's important to update the biography you share with clients. I know when you're busy, it's sometimes not a priority or something you even think of," John tapped the bios again, "but you need to do it. Make it a routine. While you may speak to your experiences in a conversation, it's helpful to keep the list of your skills current and posted. You never know which one may resonate with a client. Sometimes potential clients will do a keyword search on the internet trying to find specific expertise."

"The more you capture in words the experiences you have then, the more possibilities that potential clients may come across your biography and reach out to you. I had that happen. A potential client was looking for experts who had performed profit disgorgement analyses in connection with a government enforcement settlement. Because those words were included in my biography on the company website, the individual contacted me, and we were ultimately retained. So, to the extent you have some particular knowledge or expertise, you'll want to highlight it as you may be one of only a few who have performed those services. One specific expertise can attract additional opportunities in that space, and you could be sought as an expert."

* * *

```
-------- Original Message --------
Subject: my weekly training session with
Stephanie and Mark
From: "John"
Date: November 3
To: "Sophia Omondi"


Sophia,

What do you think of me adding the following
to my sessions with Stephanie and Mark?
Please let me know.
```

REACH OUT TO PRACTICE LEADERS AND INFORM THEM – BECOME KNOWN

While you are working on various projects, your partners or more senior practice leaders in your space may not be aware of them at a high level of detail. Even in casual conversation with your colleagues and supervisors, you can mention the work you have been performing on a project which they may find interesting, or they may know a need in their contact network, which you may be able to assist. Many senior leaders are supervising numerous professionals, so you must inform them about your experiences.

RESPOND TO INTERNAL REQUESTS FOR RELEVANT EXPERTISE

In some firms, a group email may be circulated to all the professionals looking for a particular type of knowledge and experience in connection with a potential opportunity. While some requests may contain multiple requirements, even if you believe you have the requisite expertise for some part of the request, it is worth responding with a note explicitly describing your background and interest in assisting if possible. This type of response has the effect of educating others as to your experience so they may remember this the next time an opportunity arises.

* * *

-------- Original Message --------
Subject: RE: my weekly training session with Stephanie and Mark
From: "Sophia Omondi"

Date: November 4
To: "John"

John,

I agree with you. It really comes down to projecting your capabilities and letting all know what you can do. Nothing happens if no one knows who you are and how you can help them. Please make a point of going into this in-depth with Mark and Stephanie. Especially Stephanie. She has more to offer clients than I think she sometimes believes, though it sounds like she is becoming more comfortable with a proactive and out-going approach. As you go over this with them—and I know you are already doing this—prod Mark to rein himself in a bit, have him turn inward and try different ways to get himself out there for clients and client prospects other than a 'bull in the China shop,' approach.

POINTS TO THINK ABOUT

Take a moment and reflect on what you've read and consider:

1. Have you updated your biography to include your most recent work experiences and presentations?

2. When was the last time you engaged a firm practice leader about your experience and expertise?

3. Do you have a particular experience that may set you apart from other professionals?

CHAPTER 9 –
GET YOURSELF OUT
THERE

What makes networking work is it sets up win-win situations in which all parties involved get to take something home. Networking is a sharing process. Until you understand that, you won't have much of a network."

—Earl G. Graves, Sr.

THE NEW OFFICE
REMEMBER... NETWORKING IS NOT SELLING
MENTORING SESSION – THE PROPER BALANCE OF SELF-PROMOTION VERSUS OVER-SELLING

"We're getting toward the end of my time here, and I want to ask you both to do something I think will help you. But it's not playing to your strengths. I know you may not want to do it, but trust me, it's important and worth it. Mark, I want you to do something that requires focus and is more disciplined and internal. I want you to pick a topic that fits within the industry to our client base or target market and write an article on it; you'll then distribute, post, and share. Writing an article or book or even a post on LinkedIn can raise your profile and visibility in the marketplace. The easiest method is to self-publish an extended posting or an article. And it's even better if you can write about a timely issue that has been in the news. There are groups you can join on LinkedIn that may be focused on a particular area, and you can post your article there for maximum interest. Besides online articles, there are opportunities to submit articles in certain trade magazines and journals where you can provide more content and dig a little deeper into the selected subject area. An article is a great way to show potential clients you have specific knowledge and that you can communicate ideas clearly and concisely. One little posting or article might lead to writing articles in publications with wide distribution and may get you invited to speak on panels at conferences about the subject. This is a great way to increase your visibility in the industry, and I think the discipline will help you and provide a new way for you to establish yourself and grow your network."

John turned to Stephanie, "I want you to look for opportunities to speak at events and conferences—small or large doesn't matter—or serve on a panel. The experience will open your thinking up and will kick start spontaneity, and that will help you network. Presenting a speech to an audience of potential clients is a great way to become better recognized in your area of expertise. Many people, including professionals, are intimidated by public speaking. I know that is one thing that makes you uncomfortable. But you can overcome that feeling. Giving an effective presentation requires practice, but the more you do it, the easier it gets, believe me. Again, if you adopt the philosophy, you are helping people with what you are sharing in your presentation. It becomes a more agreeable task, and when you feel that way, you can connect better with the audience. Many conference formats include panel discussions where several professionals with different expertise on a specific issue jointly present. These are an excellent way to 'work' with a client even though it is not on a retained project. Typically, some research and planning and coordination of the presentation will be required before the conference, and that provides an opportunity to exhibit your expertise and organizational skills. The close interaction involved with individuals on the panel both before and during the presentation helps you develop a bond of having worked together for a successful outcome. It may be seen a little like being in the trenches together to accomplish a common goal. In the case where you or your firm is sponsoring a panel, it is an excellent opportunity to invite potential clients to speak with you at the table. Most people would welcome the invitation and be appreciative that you gave them the chance to display their expertise as well.

"I'll work with both of you on these individual assignments; you're not in this alone. As you do this, you'll find—I think—increased interest in attending relevant conferences and meeting people related to a specific industry. And it allows you to reconnect with clients you have not seen in a while and also meet new potential clients. You can also connect with friendly competitors to get a lay of the land as to their practice and work.

"You both know the use of social media, including Facebook, LinkedIn, Instagram and Twitter has grown tremendously and continues to be a vehicle for influence and networking. It's important to be professional in your postings and remember that what you post may exist indefinitely on the internet. Sophia is a great example of this. I know that she has utilized LinkedIn over time and has over 2,000 contacts. She's written several articles and posted original analysis or commentary and received hundreds of views of them. While posting articles and comments is not the same as talking with a potential client in person, it helps to maintain your visibility in the marketplace. You never know who will reach out to you with interest."

MENTORING SESSION – HOW HELPING EARNS TRUST

"Remember my first meeting with you, where I told you about how roads last far longer than buildings? I believe that your way—your path—is created, is laid and paved, by making helping the core of your career philosophy. To do that, you must—as I've talked about probably more than you wished to hear—get out there and be involved with others. Listen to them, ask questions, and listen to the answers. That is how you learn... that's how you become visible to those who need your help. Sophia will elaborate on this when she returns, which will be soon, so expect it.

"There are certain industry organizations and associations that make sense to take part in based on your expertise and may also be an organization that has many of your potential clients as members. You should not join an organization if you are not supportive of its mission, and your only desire is to be around potential clients. A professional once indicated that he was joining and attending a community organization because it was a 'client-rich' environment. If your heart is not in it, people may soon determine that you are only participating for access to potential clients.

"There may be specific causes you are drawn to, and through that organization, you may expand your network of contacts as more people meet you and understand your profession. Volunteer and work your way up at a non-profit organization. Many cities have leadership groups that are part of a non-profit that brings together local leaders to address local issues. Having taken part in one, I found that I met people that weren't in my daily circle of contacts as they worked in government, non-profit, and foundations. A broad network will serve you well as you can become a connector of people and develop connections with people who may introduce you to other people who may be potential clients.

"While working in a consulting firm, I learned of a non-profit organization dedicated to preserving the history of the SEC and the financial services industry. As an SEC alumnus, I was interested in learning more and attended a conference the historical society was hosting. During the meeting, I met and talked with the Executive Director of the organization and expressed my interest in helping their efforts. Shortly afterward, I was contacted by the Executive Director and became more involved as a volunteer. I eventually was invited to join the Board of Trustees and worked to increase membership and raise funds. I worked my way up to being the president of the organization, and my tenure overlapped with a significant anniversary celebration. As part of the commemoration of the anniversary, the organization hosted a dinner, with 900 attendees, and I served as the master of ceremonies. I had never addressed that many people before, and it was an exciting opportunity. Over the decade I was involved in the organization, I was fortunate to meet many attorneys who would become friends and clients, and I raised my visibility during my tenure.

"School and company alumni organizations can be a valuable way to reconnect with former colleagues and schoolmates. As your fellow college students go out in the world and develop their networks, it is worth staying in touch as you never know what they may end up doing and what positions and companies they will work at. By connecting with your contact's networks, your potential for new connections grows exponentially."

* * *

```
-------- Original Message --------
Subject: Something that's proved important to
me and the growth of the business, but came
from a seed you planted/what you taught me
From: "Sophia Omondi"
Date: December 1
To: "John"
```

John,

This complements what you emailed me about your latest discussion with Mark and Stephanie.

Join Affinity Groups Where You Share Nationality, Gender

I cannot truly provide a perspective on client development tips for how a male professional would necessarily do anything differently. Still, I know that different dynamics may be in play, depending on whether the client is a man or woman. Certain groups are primarily women-oriented and focused, such as Women's

Initiative groups and others. Discuss with Mark and Stephanie how to respectfully note when meeting with clients and client prospects that there are sometimes groups or individual dynamics that may create opportunities or challenges.

POINTS TO THINK ABOUT

Take a moment and reflect on what you've read and consider:

1. When was the last time you wrote an article or presented on a panel?

2. Are you aware of the most relevant conferences for you to attend and have you attended?

3. Have you joined any community groups, non-profit organizations, or alumni networks in the last year?

4. Are you aware of organizations that your clients are members of?

ONE JOURNEY ENDS, ANOTHER BEGINS

-------- Original Message --------
Subject: my last session with Stephanie and Mark
From: "John"
Date: December 15
To: "Sophia Omondi"

Sophia,

We're all looking forward to you being back next week, but perhaps me most of all. And not because I can step away again, which I have thought about and have an idea to discuss with you. I'm looking forward to you returning so I can thank you in person. The past several months of being re-engaged in the company and industry and mentoring sharp young executives has been a tonic for me. And a great help in my own path to healing. Following is the topic from my last session with Stephanie and Mark. I think you'll find they are embracing what we've taught them. I think you'll be proud.

CHANGE SELLING INTO HELPING

SELL is a four-letter word, but so is HELP. If you will work to view client development activities as a means of helping people and not something to fear, then you can confidently grow into a successful business developer.

When we get away from the sense that we are selling something to a client and any unpleasant feelings that may be associated with selling, then the ability to grow a network and develop new business opportunities becomes a much more natural and comfortable activity to undertake. So, in looking back at my experiences in business and network development, I realized that I have performed specific actions that have worked well for me in a variety of circumstances. My efforts to continue to help people have yielded ideas and some pretty solid principles I used to start and grow the business to the point where it was an appealing and attractive enough business to merit attention as an acquisition. I've shared them in the hopes they will help all who are looking to get to the next level in their careers. These ideas may also refresh the approaches of those senior practitioners who need a re-set to their activities. You may think some of the tips provided are common sense or very fundamental and, in some ways, they may be. However, in my experience, I have found that to be successful in growing yourself and business opportunities, you will need to try a variety and combination of actions every day to see what is the most effective for your personality and what is best received by your clients.

* * *

-------- Original Message --------
Subject: At the airport, awaiting my flight home
From: "Sophia Omondi"
Date: December 21
To: "John"
To: "Mark S" <Mark.S@ePost.net>
To: "Stephanie W" <Stephanie.W@ePost.net>

John, Mark, and Stephanie,

The past eight months have been both challenging and rewarding for me personally and professionally. I've helped set the foundation for an organization I hope for decades to come will benefit the children in the nation where I was born. And I have witnessed via the many emails John and I have exchanged over the last eight months—some of which I know John has shared with you—a new foundation formed for capable junior executives in our company.

Companies… businesses… live or die by the skills of the executives that run them. Well-run companies have the odds in their favor even during tough economic times because decisions made by management prove prudent and keep it going while others fail. We all know companies cannot survive without customers and clients; both established ongoing valuable existing ones and the new that comes in and add to the stability and growth of the company.

Twenty years ago, John taught me the fundamentals of how to take care of existing clients, and best practices and principles for developing new ones by starting with a simple credo: Earn Trust… it's the basis of relationship building, and that's how sustainable businesses are born and nourished. He was gracious enough to step in so I could pursue something significant to me and has done more than just 'mind the store.' He has added value by mentoring you both, and that strengthens our company.

Mark and Stephanie, I know John has not told you yet, but even once I'm back, he has agreed to work two or three days a week with us so we can all continue to learn and benefit from his experience and wisdom. I am beyond thrilled!

They just announced the first boarding call, so I'll close for now to send this. The world is full of opportunity—something I've learned in my journey from Kenya to the United Kingdom to the United States—and I cannot wait to get back and work with you all to take our company to the next level!

See you soon,

Sophia

FINAL THOUGHTS

No matter what you do for a living and where you are in your career, there is always something new to learn and ways to improve. This guide provides insight into ways to help each other and earn the trust of our customers and clients. Collectively we can all benefit from helping each other regardless of how we do it.

Hopefully, you can relate to some of the experiences brought to life through the interactions between John, Sophia, Stephanie, and Mark. As you continue in your personal and professional life, you will learn your own lessons and discover the approaches that work best for you and your business.

While some business development situations may make you feel uncomfortable or even intimidated, it is essential to continue to break through any limitations and barriers, whether self-imposed or situational. By continuing to grow personally and professionally, you can become a more connected and more valuable advisor to better serve your customers and clients' needs.

By adjusting your outlook to view selling as a form of

helping, you may find, as I have, that your work becomes a more enriching and satisfying experience. And that it ceases to be a burden or unpleasant chore. When you become truly inspired to help your clients and are genuinely invested in their success, that is when you earn their trust. Once you have earned that trust, you have created value for yourself and your clients.

THE ANSWERS YOU'LL NEED ALONG THE WAY

You've seen these at the end of each chapter, and they're consolidated here because they are important. The following handful of questions—grouped by chapter topics—once you answer them, will help you assess whether you have a good foundation set... or if you need to do some work.

Chapter 1 – Know Your Stuff:

1. How well do you know the services your firm provides?

2. When was your most recent conversation with a colleague regarding their expertise and recent engagements?

3. When was the last time you perused your company website to learn new information?

4. Do you regularly reach out to colleagues to get an understanding of what they are working on?

Chapter 2 – In Your Client's Shoes:

1. The last time you were with a potential client, how much were you talking vs. how much were you listening?

2. Do you clarify and confirm with the potential client what services they are specifically looking for?

3. How often do you try to put yourself in the shoes of the client and expect what they may ask or say?

Chapter 3 – Establishing Trust & Delivering On It:

1. When was the last time you engaged with a client on non-business issues?

2. How often do you see a client outside of the specific engagement you worked on together?

3. Do you understand what outside interests your clients have?

Chapter 4 – Connecting Through Socialization:

1. When was the last time you invited a client out to an event?

2. Are you aware of events at your firm where you could invite clients?

3. What was the last event you attended with a client?

4. How often do you stay in touch with the clients you have worked with?

Chapter 5 – Maintain Contact With Clients:

1. What do you do to maintain contact with clients?

2. How often do you reach out to your clients?

3. Have you sent a client an article or news story in the last month?

Chapter 6 – Spend More Time On Existing Clients:

1. What have you done recently to stay in touch with your best clients?

2. When was the last time you made an introduction to a client of someone who may help their business?

3. Have you provided any "free advice" to a good client recently?

4. When was the last time a good client introduced you to some of their colleagues?

Chapter 7 – Make New Contacts:

1. What is the size of your network in terms of contacts?

2. How much has your network grown since the same time last year?

3. What steps have you taken in the last three months to increase your network?

4. How do you use social media to expand your contacts?

Chapter 8 – Marketing Your Skills:

1. Have you updated your biography to include your

most recent work experiences and presentations?

2. When was the last time you engaged a firm practice leader about your experience and expertise?

3. Do you have a particular experience that may set you apart from other professionals?

Chapter 9 – Get Yourself Out There:

1. When was the last time you wrote an article or presented on a panel?

2. Are you aware of the most relevant conferences for you to attend, and have you attended?

3. Have you joined any community groups, non-profit organizations, or alumni networks in the last year?

4. Are you aware of organizations that your clients are members of?

ABOUT THE AUTHOR

James W. "Jim" Barratt is a business professional with over 30 years of professional services industry experience. He is a Certified Public Accountant and has provided services to clients around the world in the areas of auditing, consulting, and government service. Jim has worked in many countries and has presented on a variety of issues at various conferences, webcasts, and live training. Jim has learned from many of the leading professional services practitioners and has served as a mentor to many staff people. He has worked at firms that were start-ups to large global entities. He has led and grown several professional services practices from scratch. In addition to his professional career, Jim has actively been involved with and served on the board of many non-profit entities over his lifetime. He enjoys traveling the world, meeting new people, and learning about cultures and societies. In both his professional and personal capacity, at his core, he enjoys helping people.

www.ingramcontent.com/pod-product-compliance
Lightning Source LLC
Chambersburg PA
CBHW032009190326
41520CB00007B/410